A COLUMBUS OF SPACE

the notebook edition

Colour the Classics
xoxo

For

You

xoxo

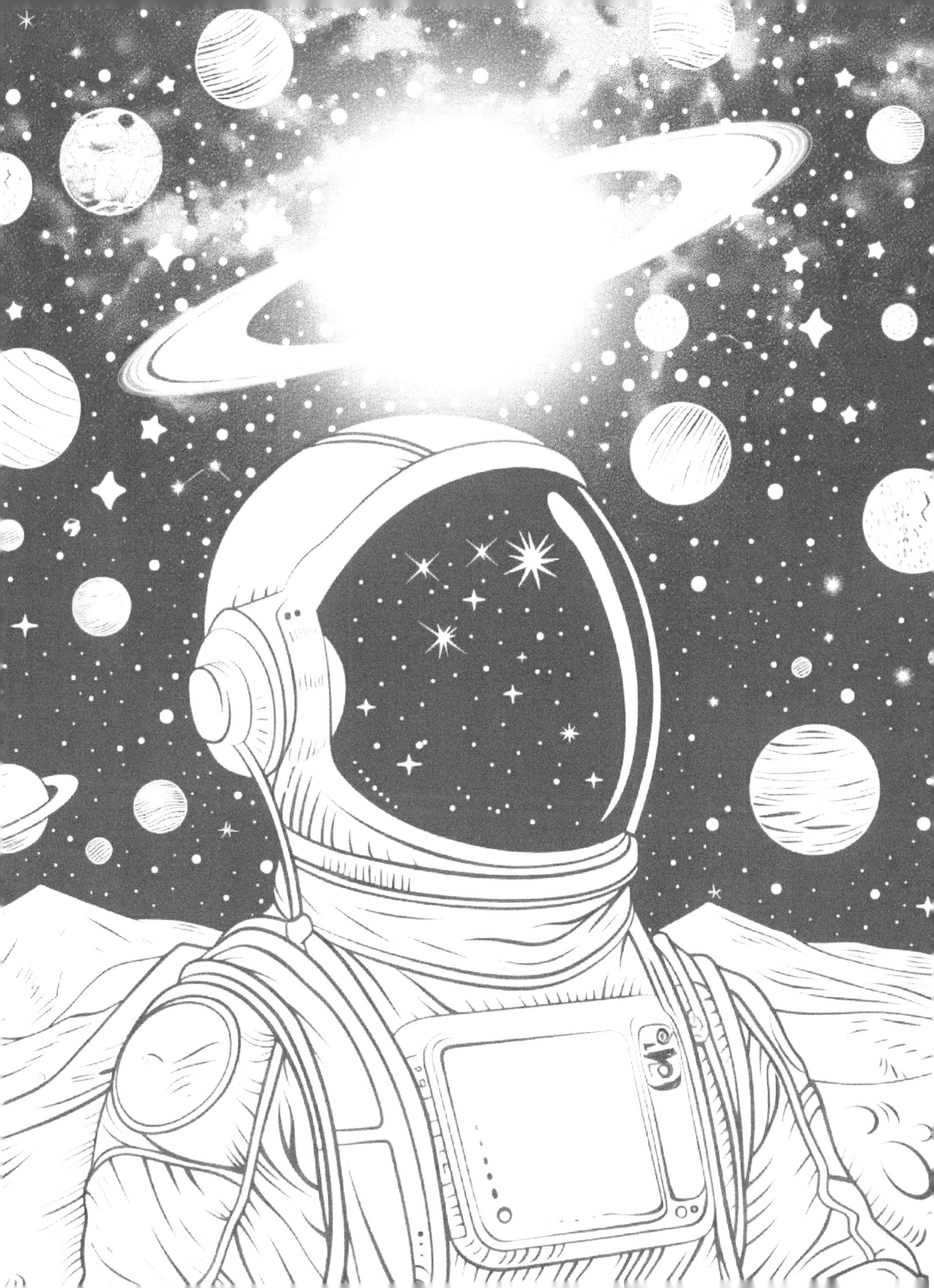

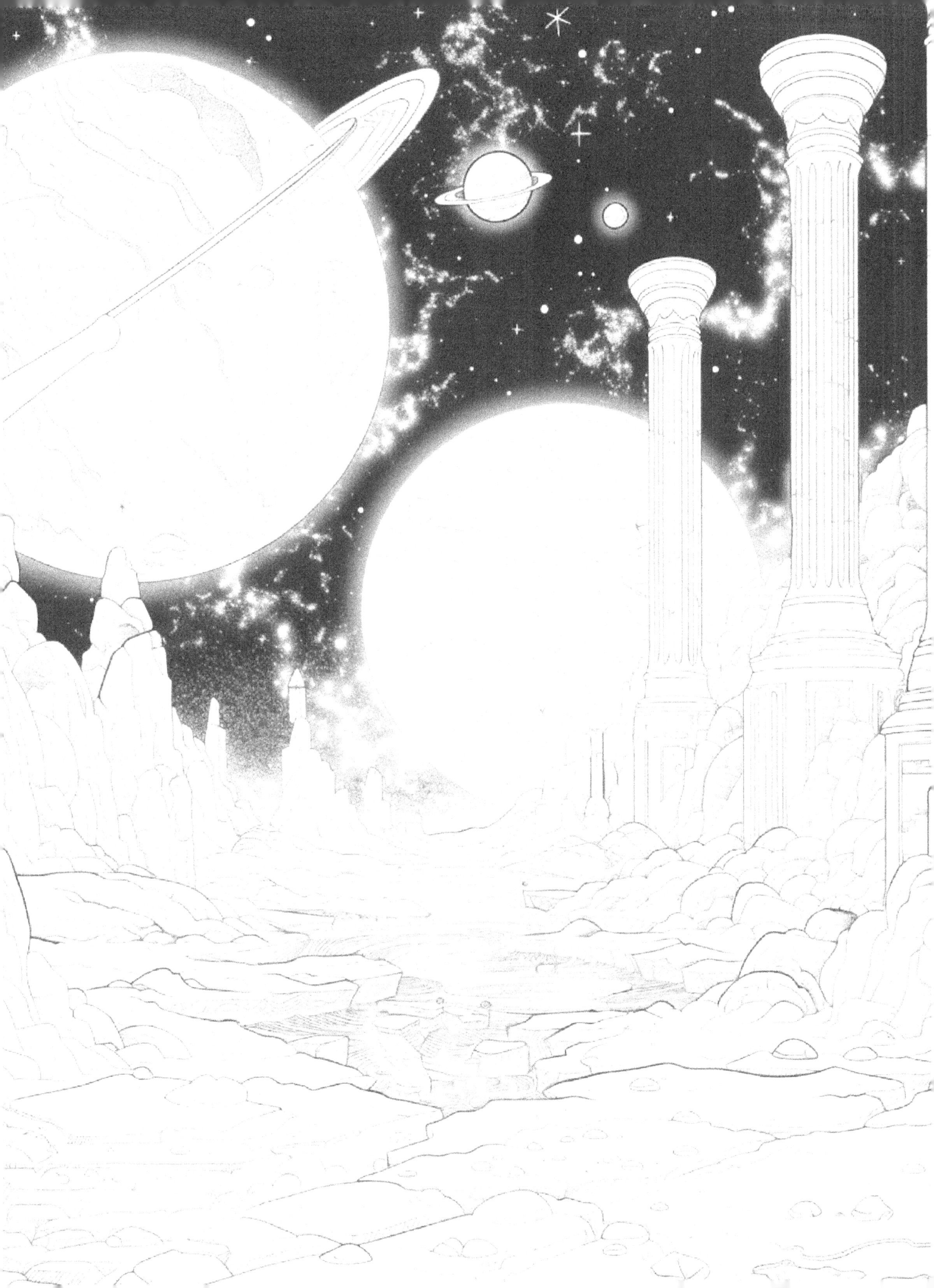

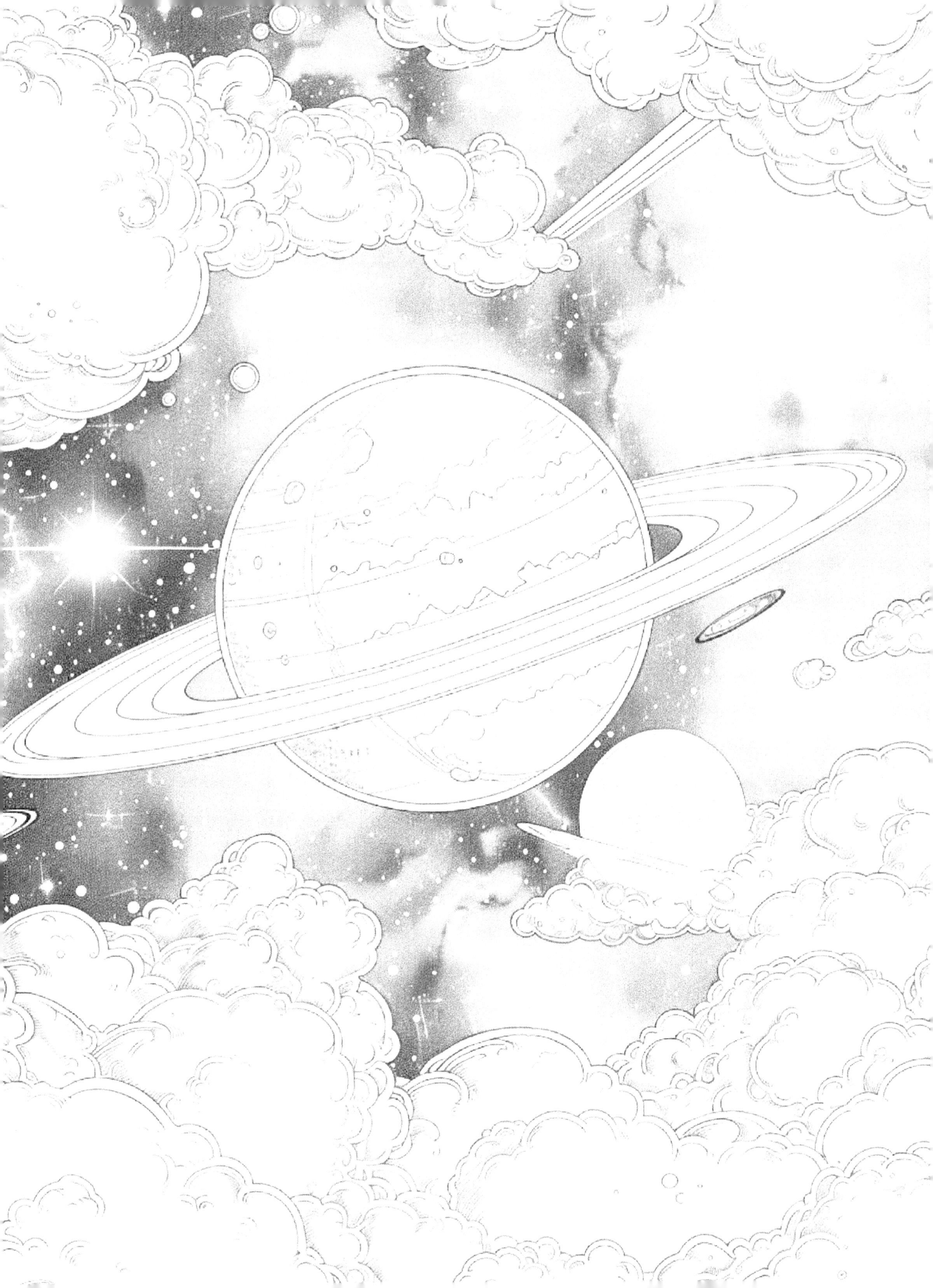

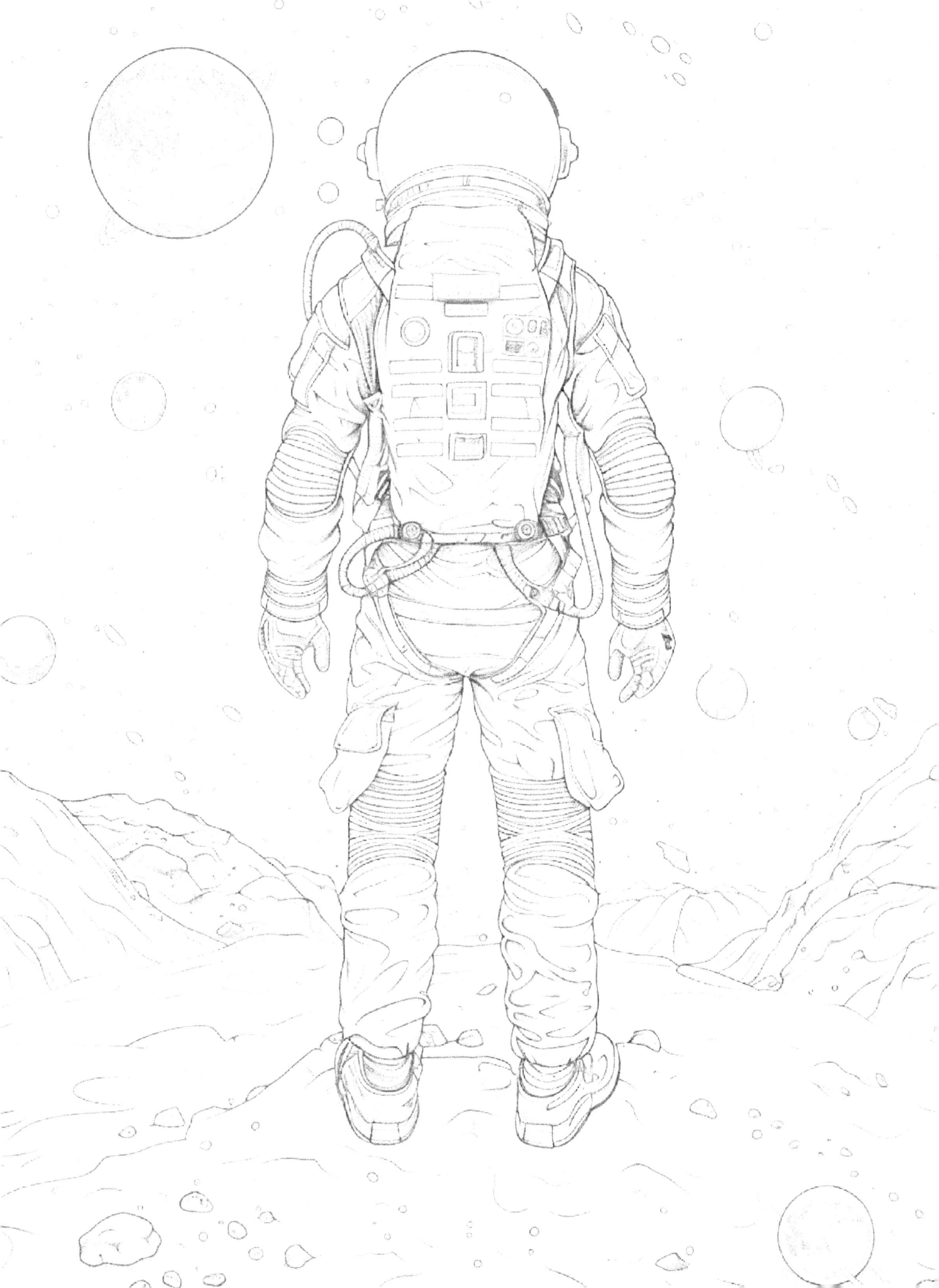

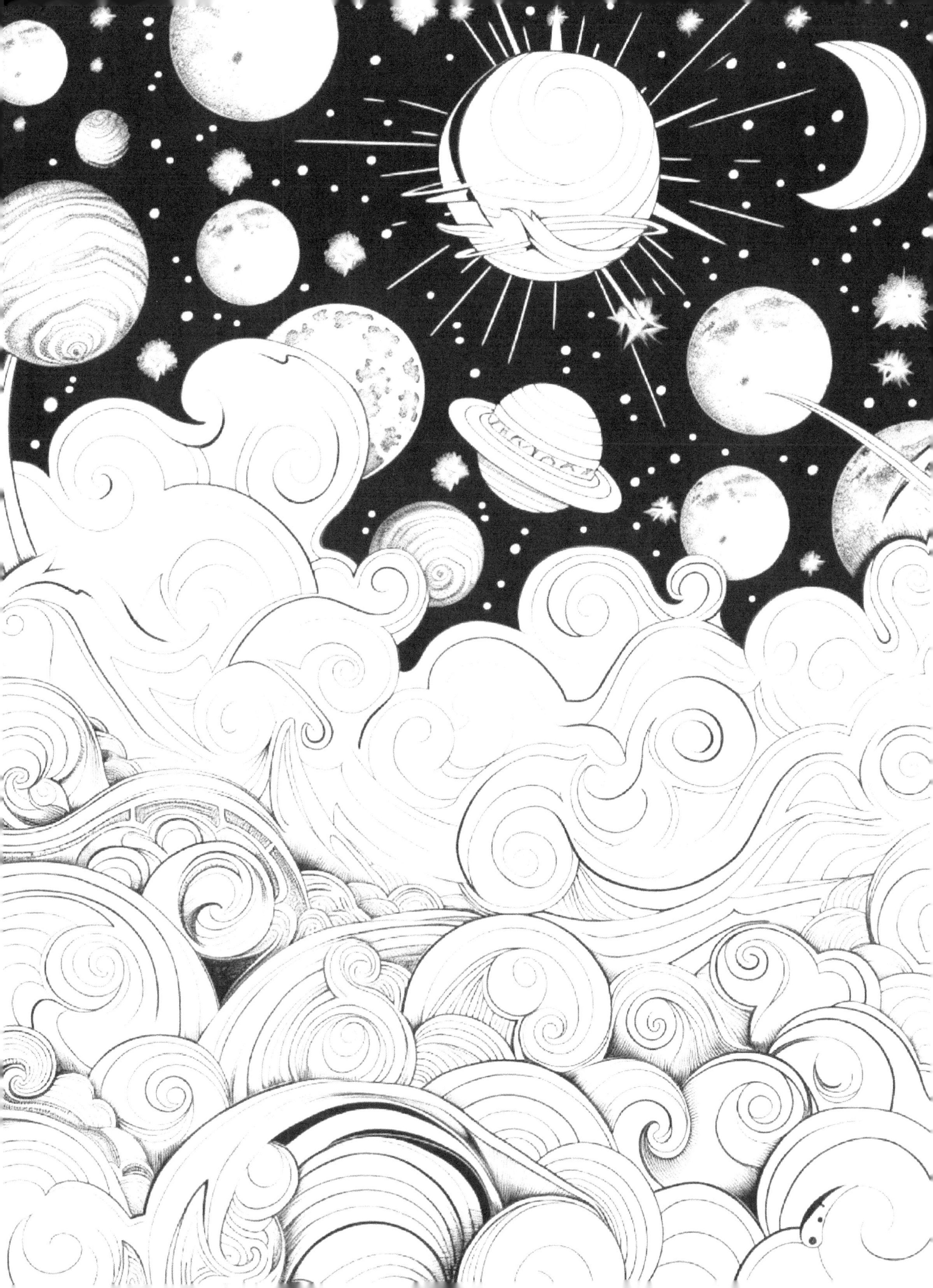

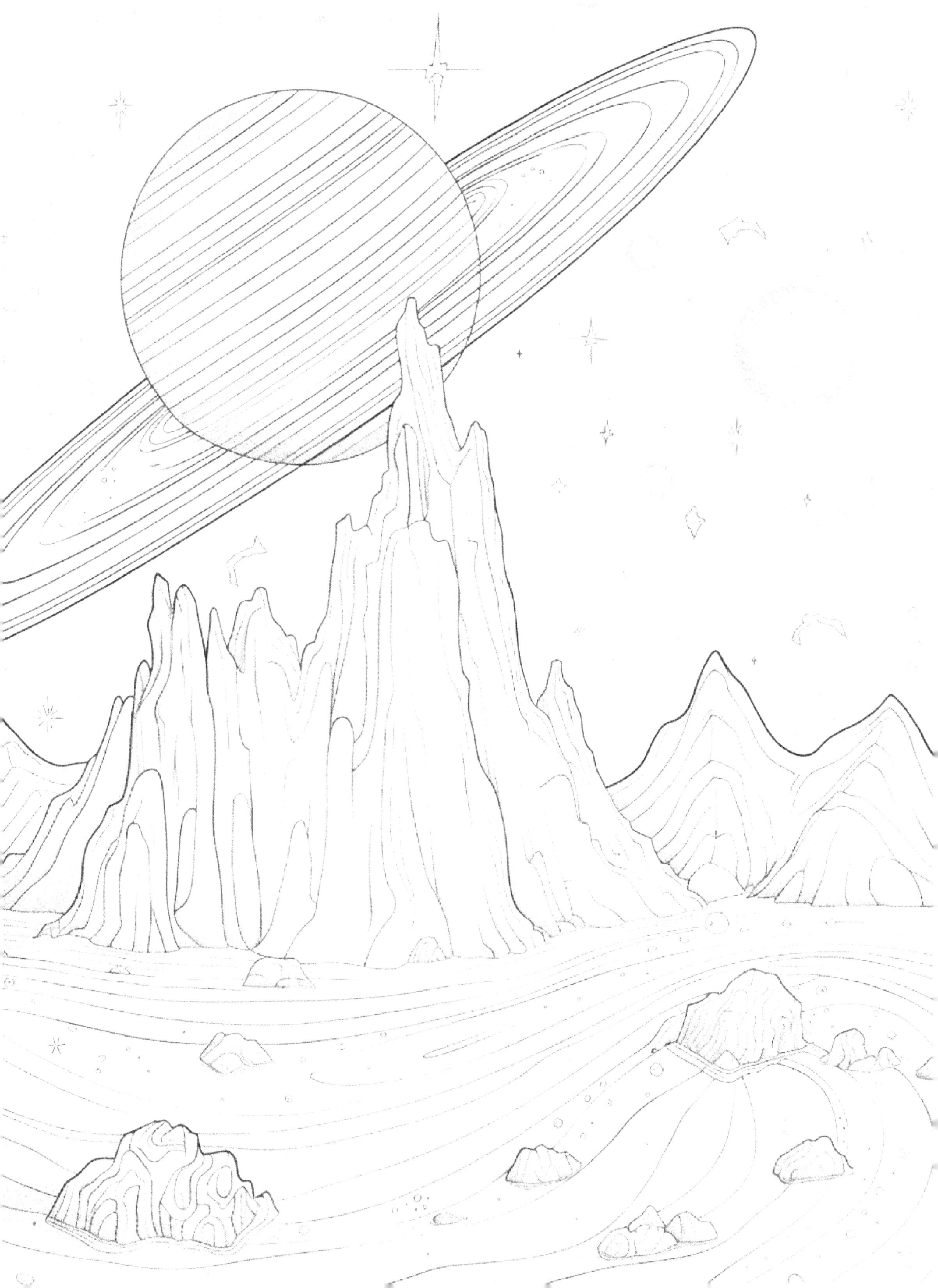

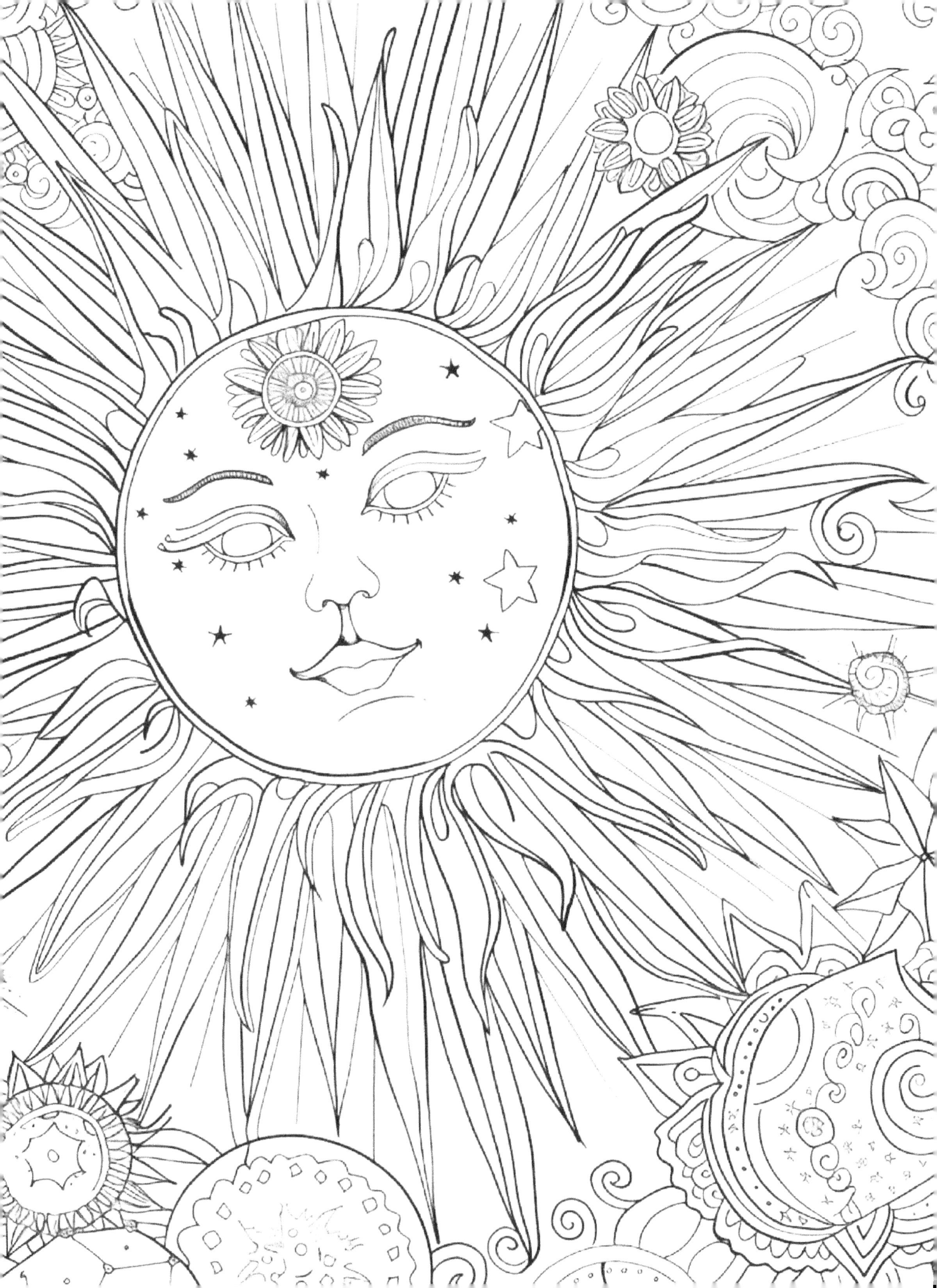

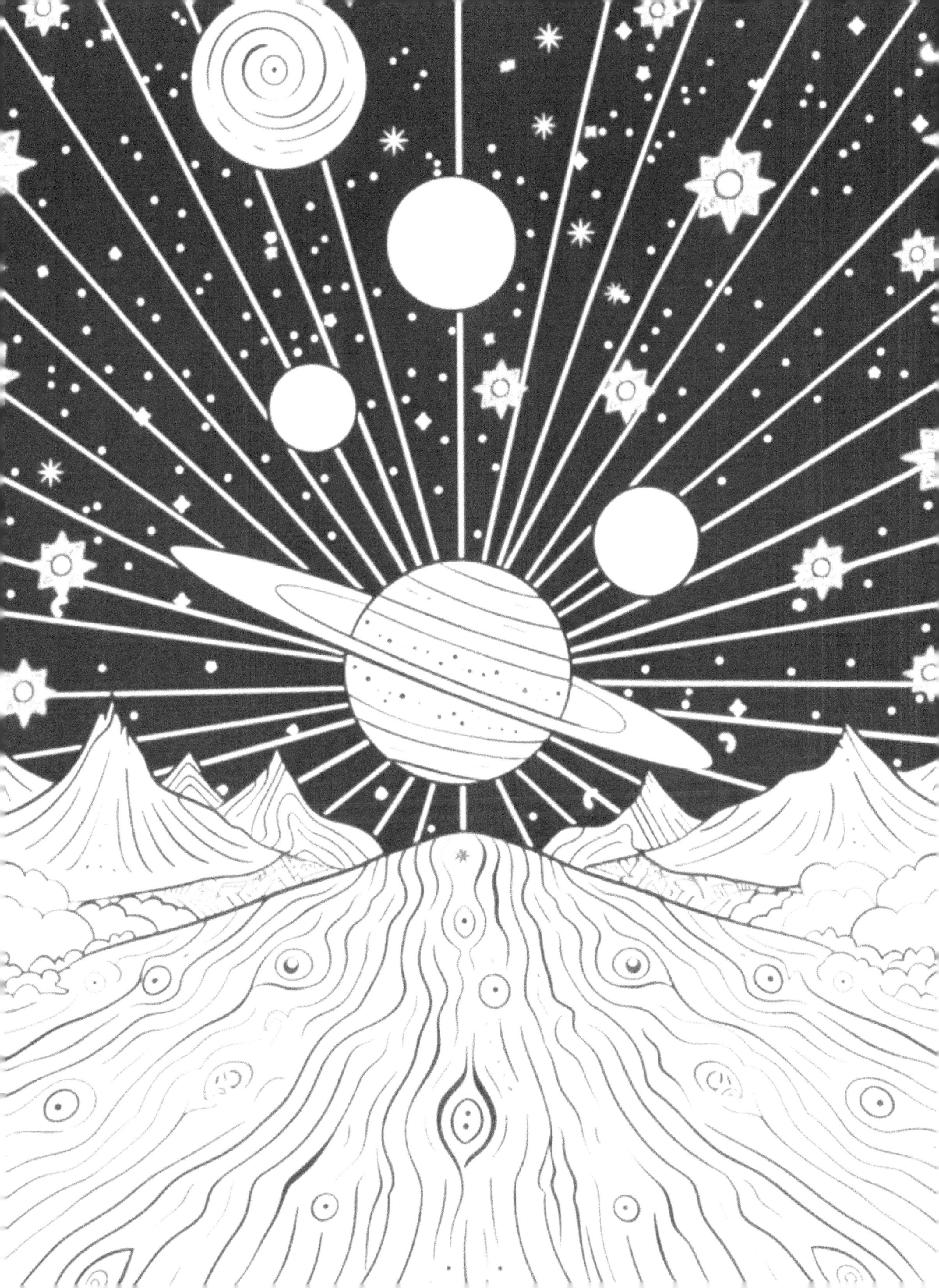

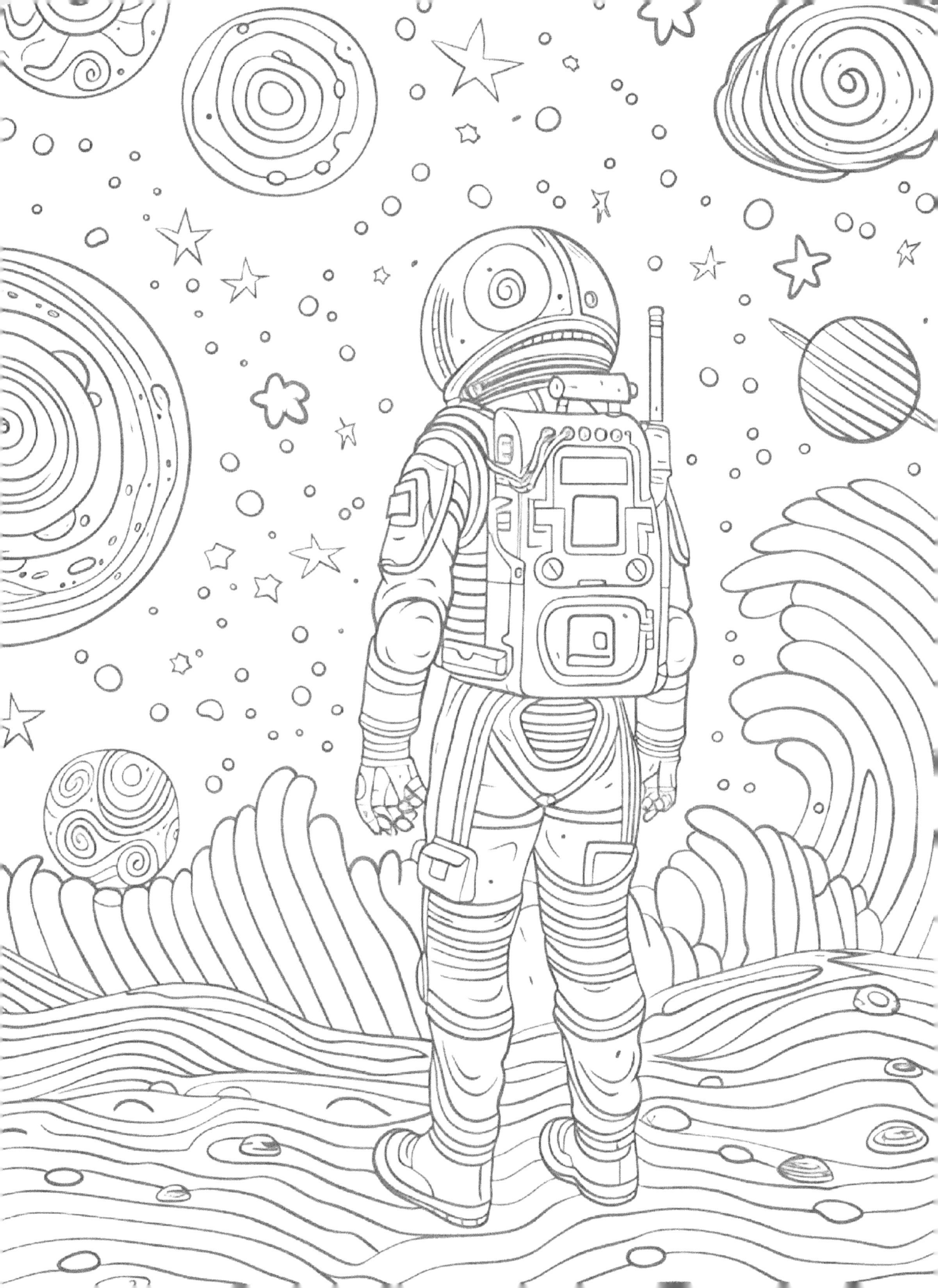

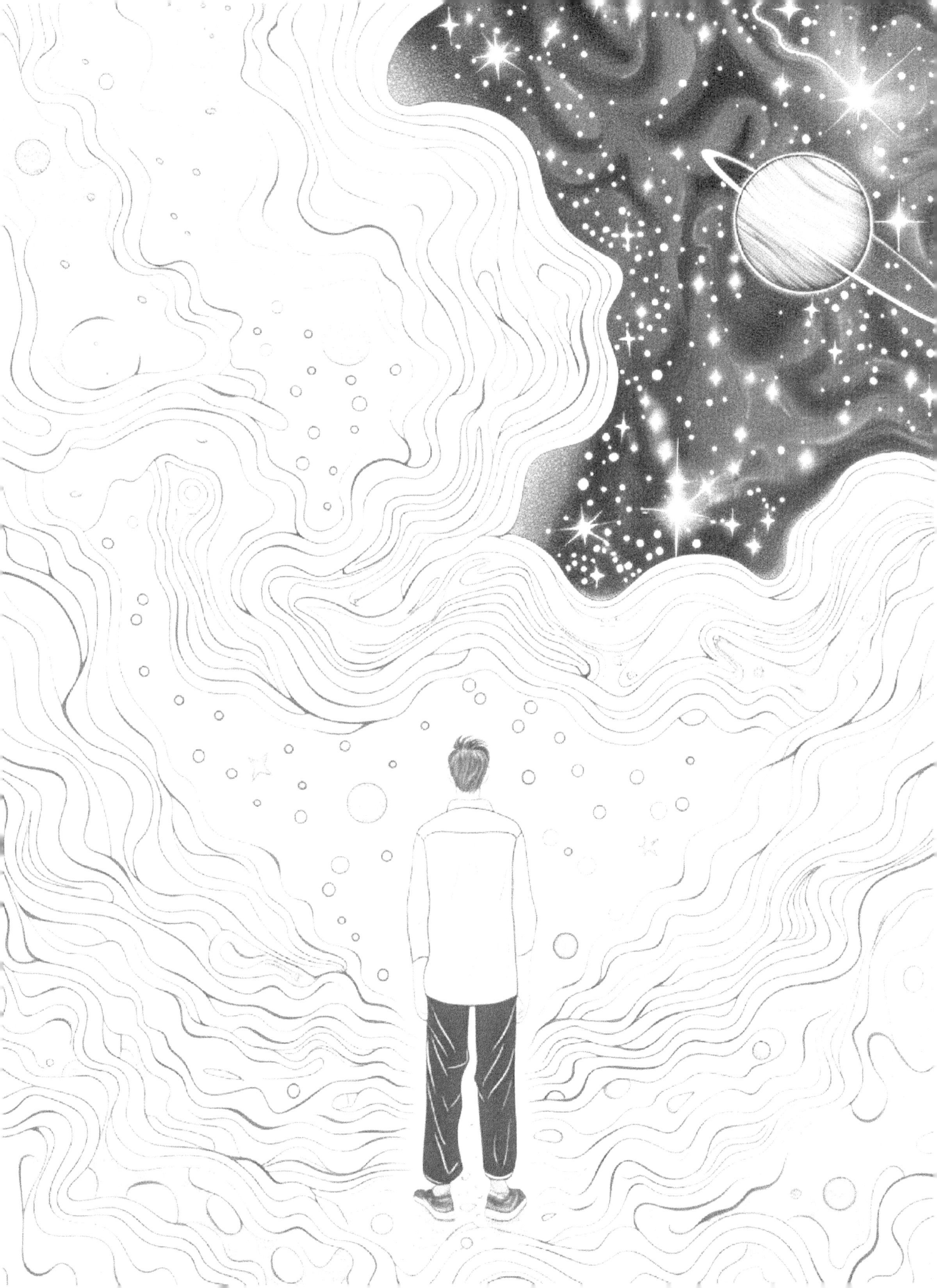

The End